old
bags

taking a stand

First Printing: 2015
ISBN-13: 978-0692510629
old bags LLC
www.oldbagsproject.com

Ordering Information:
Books may be ordered at the website: **oldbagsproject.com**

created by
Faith Baum and Lori Petchers

Liz Harvey, photographer

Published by OLD BAGS LLC
oldbagsproject.com

To all of the women
who agreed to be
"bagged"
for this project.

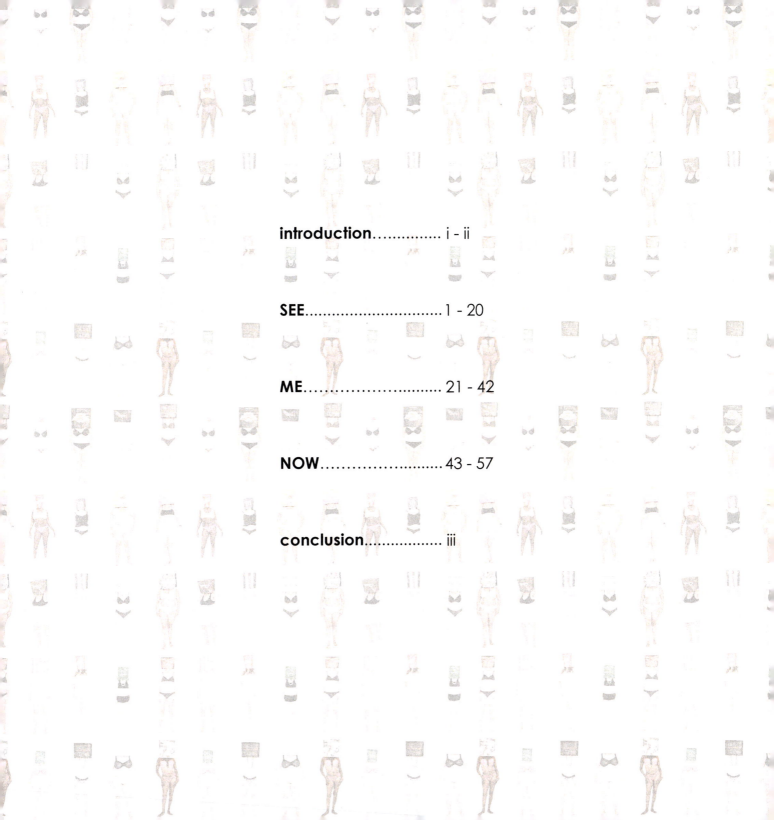

introduction

OLD BAGS TAKING A STAND is the culmination of a five-year, multidisciplinary project exploring the reality of being a middle-aged American woman through documentary, visual art, and social media. This book combines these three facets to create a reading experience intended to be empowering, funny, and universal.

Many postmenopausal women, like ourselves, feel that we are becoming irrelevant in a youth-fixated society at the exact time of our lives when we have achieved a sense of who we are and what we want from our lives. This contradiction offers the opportunity for public discourse about the stereotypes of female aging.

OLD BAGS TAKING A STAND provides the reader with thoughts culled from countless interviews with middle-aged women. The book uses their words to represent major areas of interest to this segment of society: how they feel they are seen by others, how they perceive themselves, and how they have grown into self-acceptance through their experiences. These themes are divided into three chapters; **See**, **Me**, and **Now**.

The women's words are accompanied by photographic images that are irreverent and compelling. Poking fun at consumerism and mockingly neutralizing a stale insult, older women from diverse backgrounds take a stand.

The women strip down to their underwear and pose in front of the camera with shopping bags over their heads. They can't look back at you to see your reaction to their waist lines, hips, C-sections, appendectomy scars, and whatever else life has dealt them. The bags also prevent you, the viewer, from shifting your gaze to their faces as a refuge from the forbidden view of their "not-so-young anymore" bodies. Despite the tsunami of current visual information, the reality of the middle-aged woman's body is rarely seen except in advertisements about lifting, squashing, incising, creaming, and hiding.

OLD BAGS TAKING A STAND is <u>not</u> a soap commercial about how everyone is beautiful. It <u>is</u> a statement about refusing to allow an anti-aging culture to have the last word about who we are and our place in American society.

This book presents real bodies and real viewpoints. The only actual old bags come from the stores in which we shop.

SEE ME NOW

Faith Baum and Lori Petchers, 2015

SEE

A common theme expressed during the interviews with middle-aged women was their sense of not being seen anymore. For some it caused sadness, as it was a clear indication of lost youth and beauty. For many, reaching middle age was a relief. They enjoyed a feeling of release by virtue of not being seen. Other women refused to embrace the notion of "invisibility." They saw it as an opportunity for re-invention in order to remain visible. Our feelings about how we are viewed by others (or not seen), change in midlife.

How do people SEE us?

"Well, one of the things that happens is that as soon as you're **not fertile** anymore, men look at you differently. It's like you **become invisible.** It's strange but in some ways it's also **liberating.** You can be a crazy old lady if you want. You can stand on the street corner and say, 'That's a stop sign there!' I think it's **hard-wired into humans** that once you're not fertile, you somehow don't exist."

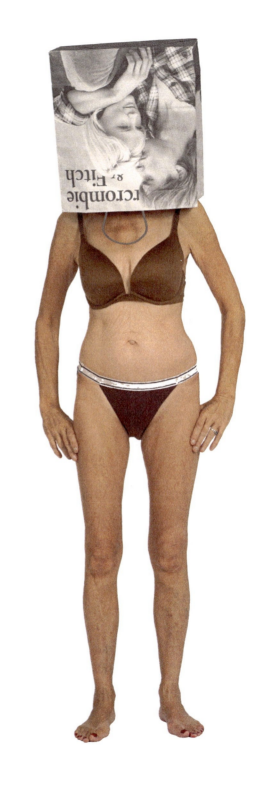

"There's definitely a time when you know that you can still **turn heads.** You're noticed, even by other women. Then that starts to go and you start having **less of a presence.** That happens in your thirties. It doesn't wait until **menopause.** You start to feel **replaced.** That sense of having the key to the city, well, you're giving it to somebody else."

"I think as women, especially in our society, there is **a lot of importance placed upon how people see you**. Now, if I were isolated and alone, I would be okay with myself."

"Even if we are in-shape and skinny, we do not look like a 25-year-old. We **do not make peace** with that. We look in mirrors and we want the surgical cosmetic stuff. **Nobody has a clue about what looking good is for a middle-aged woman."**

"So, the thought that I go places and the **guy** that passed me doesn't even look twice anymore is **disconcerting**. It's also the reality. But I am the same and I still really look men over. If I were single, I would definitely be interested in a relationship with a man again, a **sexual relationship.**"

"My husband still desires me."

"Sometimes when I'm walking down the street, I look into a storefront and I see a **reflection.** It's my **mother** in the glass. Then I am shocked because **that old lady is me!"**

"I am really **afraid** that I am going to get pushed out of my **job.** So I **colored my hair** and I got these **funky glasses** so that no one really knows my age. I am not seen as hip and funny anymore. I guess this is **ageism** but somehow it seems worse for women than men."

"I think about the perception of what **everybody thinks is young.** Every time you see somebody, they've had work done. So your perception is that's **the way you are supposed to look."**

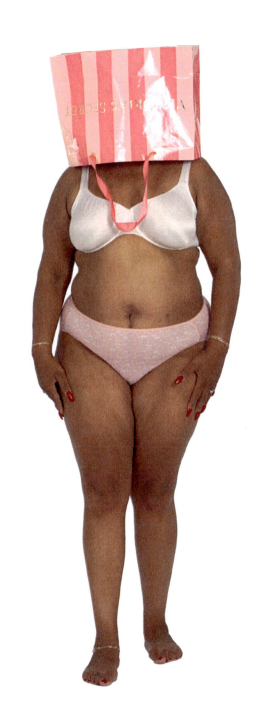

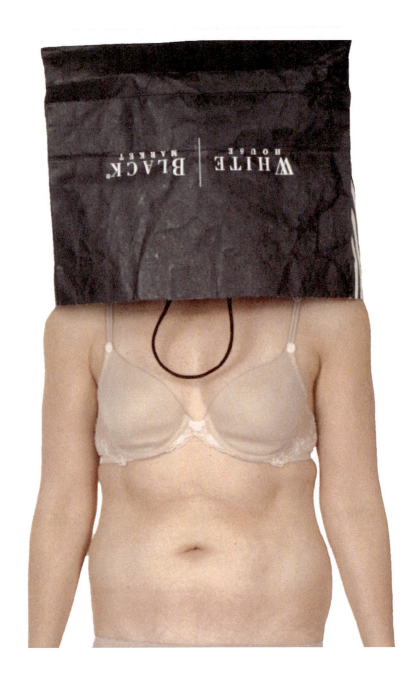

10

"It's hard for the women who live by their **youth** and their **youth** is their only thing. It all goes away, and, believe me honey, this came very fast, 61?... really???"

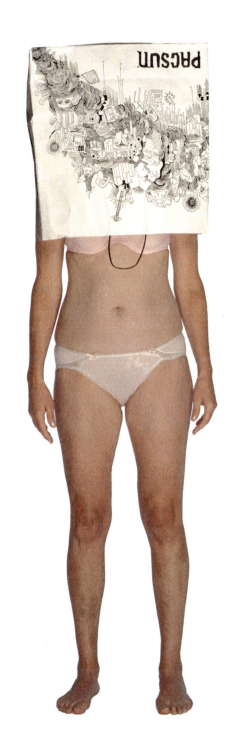

"I'm sick of women talking about feeling **invisible.** You are only as invisible as you feel. **I'm 52 and I don't look it... I look good."**

"I hate when someone says **'You don't look 63!'** What am I supposed to say, thank you? **I want to look my age and be told that I look good."**

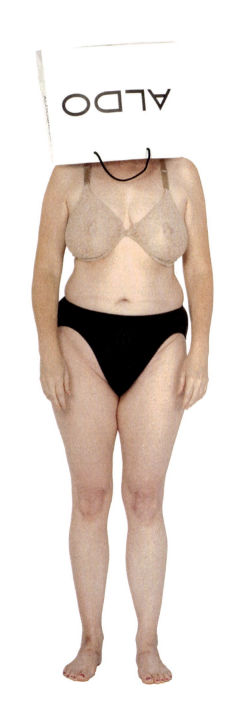

"I've become very conscious of **how I feel as a woman** who is well over the **age of 35.** There are instances where I feel **invisible.** Whether it's due to the fact that I get called **'Ma'am'** or ... I just see it very clearly... It's the young women that are looked at by men. It's the young women, not the middle-aged ones, who are regarded as paragons of beauty. There's such an **emphasis placed on good looks** and being beautiful and fit. I think that women at this age have a really hard time grappling with the **reality of aging,** with respect to how the **culture values youth** and youthful beauty rather than wisdom, experience, and character."

"I can't understand why more **middle-aged** women aren't **criminals.** We probably could get away with anything because **nobody notices us."**

ME

Many middle-aged women speak about not recognizing their own reflections and about the disconnect between how they feel inside and what their bodies have become. Some react to an altered appearance with plastic surgery or turn to shopping for "anti-aging" cosmetics and "youthful" clothing - anything to connect their outer and inner selves. Other women comfortably sit in their new physiques, but the emotional changes of the empty nest, failing marriage, or stalled career force them to re-define their identity and sense of self. In this pursuit of their personal identity, the women answer the question:

How do I perceive ME ?

"You look at yourself in the **mirror** and you say, **'My god, whose face is this?** Where did this face come from?' "

"Moisturizer is my friend."

"I swear I have more **lotions** and **potions** than anyone. I can spend more time in that aisle than anybody else in the world. I read all the labels thinking, 'Hmmmm, which one of these is gonna be best?' "

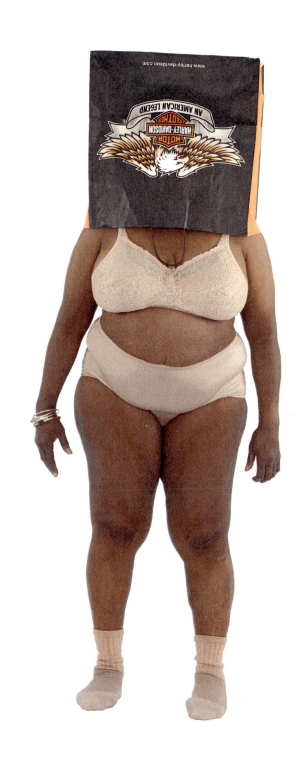

"We're all **vain.** I don't think there's anything wrong with that, but I wouldn't take my vanity so far as to get **Botox** or anything like that. I think that's absolutely ridiculous."

"In terms of **Botox ...** that's an issue I struggle with. How much am I going to do? **What will I be comfortable with?"**

"I really thought about having a tummy tuck. A lot of people would look at me and say, 'you don't need a tummy tuck.' But what's my self-image? What am I comfortable with? **I would love to have a tummy tuck.** Then I get some information about the type of surgery. It's major surgery! I weighed the risks/rewards ... **I am not doing a tummy tuck!"**

"**Shopping** for flattering clothes that don't **cinch** my nebulous **waist**, reveal my **veined legs**, or showcase my vague **lumps** has become the most demanding enterprise of my fifties. Some of my most creative thinking has gone into putting together **flattering outfits.** Few of us are athletes."

"**There's gotta be something between skinny jeans and mom jeans.**"

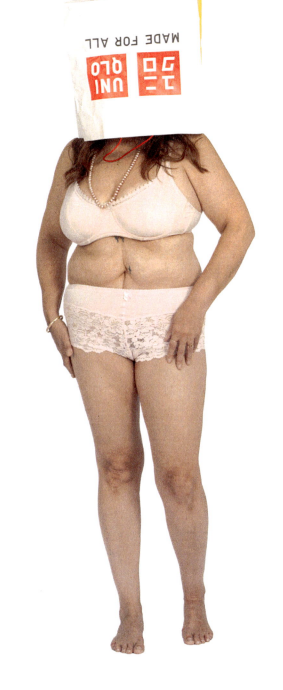

 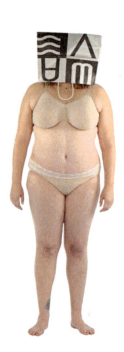

"My greatest fear is losing my brain. **My whole identity is my brain.**"

"I don't **dye my hair.** There's a little **gray** starting, and, at first, I was gonna **embrace** it ... and then I found myself **pulling** them out."

"Okay, my neck. I'm not crazy about my neck. I look at it and go, **'Wouldn't it look better if ... ?'** "

"Sixty was hard. I had my last child at 44. I have been **parenting most of my life.** I had my first child when I was 19. I was **busy.** I did not have the time to think about getting older. Turning 60 was a rude awakening. I was crying, **'It's gone, it's over!' "**

"I'm really struggling with the fact that my **kids** are growing up and **leaving** and I'm going to have an **empty nest.** People say, 'Oh, now you can finish that book you started! You can travel and do all the things you want to do.' Well, yeah, I could do those things and probably will but I am still going to **miss that part of my life** that I've invested 22 years in. It's never over. I don't think we ever stop parenting, but **the way I parent will change** and it's the unknown for me. It's kind of **scary."**

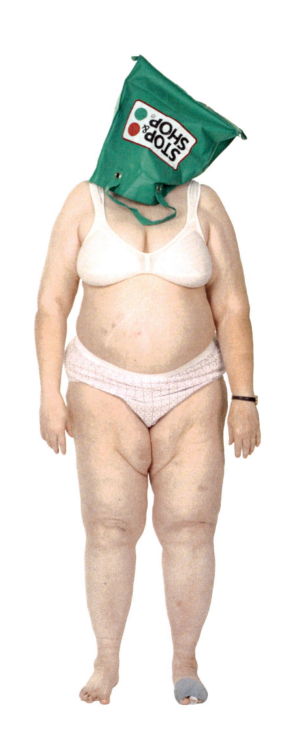

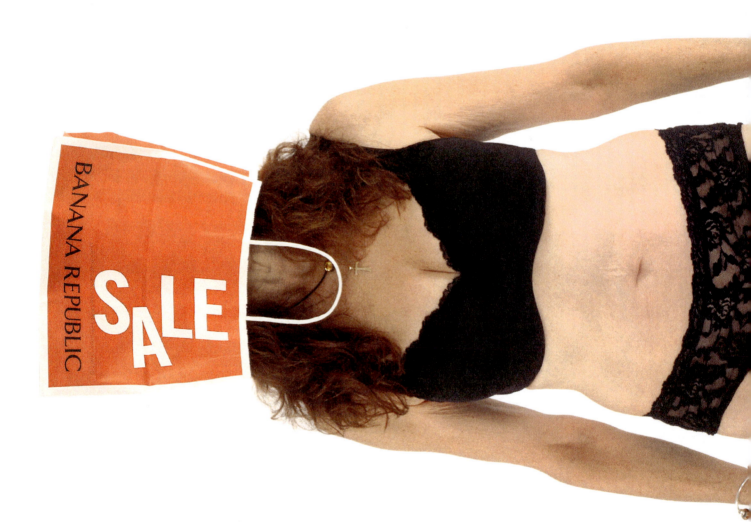

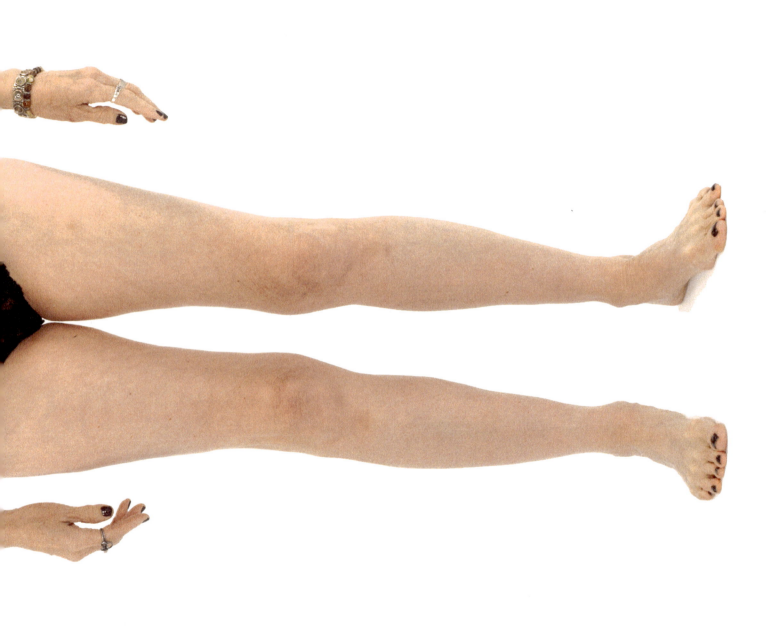

"**Aging** is something that happens to other people. I cannot tell you how it **hit me.** I didn't like 30, I didn't like 40, but 50 slammed me in the face. The **mortality** thing comes into play. You are well **past halfway.** Your outlook changes. I mean mine has. **I even lie about my age to the Stairmaster.** I put in 45 because I refuse to put in 50. I will always put in 45."

"I don't really view myself as one of those **pretty girls.** I'm kind of average, **a plain Jane.** But I've always been so thin and now, no matter what I do, I've **put on some pounds.** One minute, I'm **appalled,** 'Oh my god, I cannot believe it' , and then, the next minute, I'm like, 'part of this is just the **aging process.'** You get these **certain areas** that collect the fat better than others."

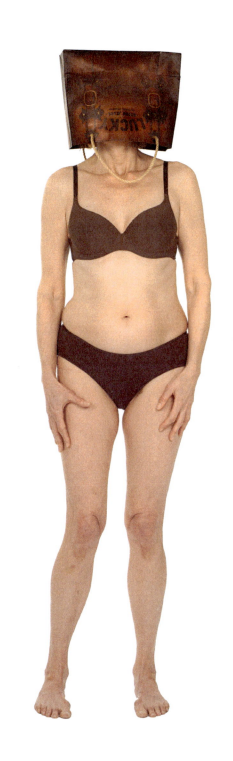

"I'm okay with where I am now but I miss **the chaos and purpose** of when the kids were **young.** I went back for **another degree."**

"I was always **self-conscious** about my **body;** it wasn't right, it wasn't this, it wasn't that. And, when I look back on what it looked like, I would do anything to have it back today. So it's difficult to watch **things change** right before my eyes. It just blows me away."

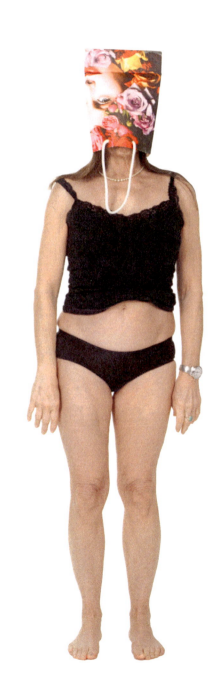

"I've really started thinking about that archetypical story about **Snow White** and her **Evil Stepmother.** When I was a **girl,** I was Snow White. Now, as a **woman of a certain age,** being over 50, I'm very conscious of having crossed the line. I am moving in the direction of either becoming the Evil Stepmother, who hates the young, beautiful, and nubile girls, or becoming the flip side of the Evil Stepmother, which is the **wise crone.** The wise woman knows how to conjure healing energy and she understands the wisdom of going through each **stage of life**. Every stage of life offers a different perspective, but **our society is still very youth oriented."**

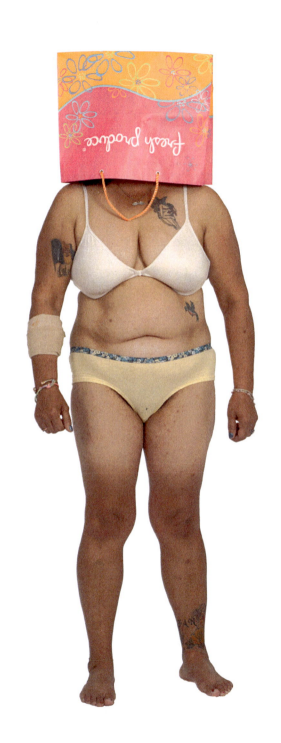

NOW

There are ways in which American society views the middle-aged women and ways in which we perceive ourselves. Most of the women that were interviewed recognized these sometimes opposing views. They reacted with a desire to come to terms with the realities of aging and an interest in becoming clearer about their own identities.

Where do we stand NOW ?

"In all my craziness, I feel like now is the time for me to **learn** and to really **do what I want to do**. My time is filled with that rather than, 'Oh, I wonder how somebody else sees me.' "

"I am 53 in my **head** and 53 in my **body.** I probably have 58 or 59 year-old **wrinkles** around my eyes. That's it... I don't care. **Frankly, I don't care.**"

"We don't get rid of all the **baggage.** I like to tell everyone, we all have baggage, but I just have a carry-on. **I got rid of the heavy stuff.**"

"In comparison to middle age, youth is almost like an illness to be endured. Now **I can focus** on the important things like my intellect, love, a relationship. Only now do I feel like I can give myself completely to a man. Because **I am the most complete I've ever been and may ever be.**"

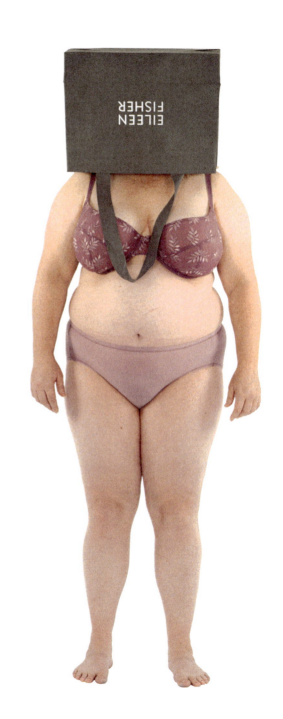

"It's a **paradox** at this age. On the one hand, I have more patience and greater determination and, on the other hand, I have less **patience**. I have become more exacting with myself by saying 'Okay, cut to the chase and just do it.' **I don't have the luxury of time that I had when I was 25.**"

"I got to a point where I didn't want to be **closeted** anymore. I was tired of leading a double life and I wanted **to be out** in the worst way. When I finally did that, there was such a **tremendous gush of relief**. I started to realize who I really was and was so proud of myself. It was very exciting and very **empowering.** Everything happened at once."

"After **menopause**, your **sexuality** isn't so plugged into procuring a mate, making babies and ensuring you have a safe nest. You're beyond that. It's a mixed blessing. **It allows you to focus.**"

"I was doing my **resume** and I realized that everything I did to raise my kids prepared me to **run a corporation.** I can do anything as long as I have a good **computer person to back me up.**"

"I don't think I'm supposed to parent my adult children anymore and I don't want to."

"Identity is my **midlife transition.** Who am I? I am no longer young. I am not actively mothering anymore. I am married. I am wiser and more comfortable in my body than I was. At least for fleeting moments, **I am moving forward."**

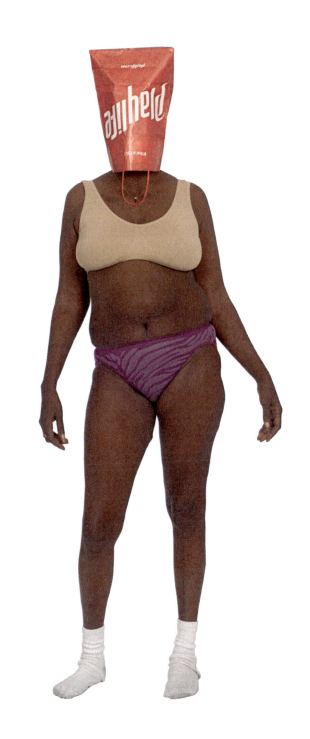

"Invisible? I felt invisible **before middle age.** I was so **stressed out** ...dinners to cook every night, child-care worries, and feeling guilty because I'm at work and the kids are home sick. I was invisible before. **Now I am more me;** no more guilt, no more exhaustion."

"Because I knew what direction I wanted to go, I started **taking better care of myself.** I started saying no to people a little bit more, started doing work on some old trauma stuff. **I ate a lot of soybeans.** That didn't work out too well...I don't recommend it. Gave me a **big bellyache."**

"At this age, you get your **validation from other women** who are going through the same thing. I think it helps if you can **talk** about it and **laugh** about it. Everybody is thinking that they're the only ones that are looking in the mirror. Everything is sagging and there are rings under the eyes and you're looking at the jowls. If you're **on the same page** with people, it diffuses it. I think if you talk about it, it's not this great horrible scary elephant in the center of the room."

"I have a **better sense of humor** about who I am. Now, if something doesn't work out, I just chalk it up and **go onto the next thing.**"

"I definitely have my **ups and downs. My introspection** is a little more dominant. I spend more time making comparisons between now and then. Maybe it's not all that different but now I **have more time and information** to think about it. Ten or fifteen years ago I would have been held back by 'that's not okay.' Now I'm more inclined to say 'whatever.' **Life is short.** It is like a reward for getting to this point. I think a lot of women have this sort of **epiphany**, like an **awakening** of sorts. I don't know if it is the hormones subsiding or whether you've accumulated enough history, but your **mind frees up** and you can say **'I think I'll do that.'** "

conclusion

This book was created by so many women, nameless and faceless but spirited and insightful. They are members of the baby boom generation who are coping with the reality of getting older, and old has become an insult in America.

If we place too much value on the importance of youth, we allow ourselves to be marginalized. If we define ourselves solely by our appearance, we lose the benefits of the wisdom that time has presented us. If we become slaves of the consumer culture, we buy a message that ultimately limits our potential. If we see ourselves as "less than," then others won't see us at all. It's important for ourselves and for future generations that the naked truth about female midlife is revealed. Take a stand.

SEE US NOW

continue the discussion at
oldbagsproject.com

acknowledgements

Thanks to Karen Kwass, Sophie Kwass, Maryrose McGowan, Lucy McGing, Meredith Reuben, Geraldine Baum, Ryan Odinak, Linda Quinn, Denise Farley, Robbin Zella, Jasmine Chang, Regina Baena Madwed, Capitol Photo Interactive, Helen Kauder, Kyle Sklar, Artspace New Haven, Rhode Island School of Design Photography Department, Laura Einstein, Ilona Levine, Susan Reinhart, the Petchers Family, Joe Plotkin, Odile Isralson, Sasha Ingber, Felicia Watson, Ian Adamson, Bruce Kushnick, and Crys Moore.